W9-CCD-999

I Am a Dancer

Pat Lowery Collins

illustrations by

Mark Graham

Ⓜ Millbrook Press · Minneapolis

To Patricia Conway —PL

To Elena —MG

Text copyright © 2008 by Pat Lowery Collins
Illustrations copyright © 2008 by Mark Graham

Millbrook Press
A division of Lerner Publishing Group, Inc.
241 First Avenue North
Minneapolis, MN 55401 U.S.A.

Website address: www.lernerbooks.com

Library of Congress Cataloging-in-Publication Data

Collins, Pat Lowery.
    I am a dancer / by Pat Lowery Collins ; illustrated by Mark Graham.
      p.   cm. — (Millbrook picture books)
    ISBN 978–0–8225–6369–3 (lib. bdg. : alk. paper)
    1. Dance—Juvenile literature. 2. Dancers—Juvenile literature. 3. Picture
books for children. I. Graham, Mark, 1952– ill. II. Title.
GV1596.5.C65 2008
792.62—dc22   2007021885

Manufactured in the United States of America
1 2 3 4 5 6 – DP – 13 12 11 10 09 08

I am a dancer each morning
as I shimmy out of bed,

zip down the banister,

or skip stairs.

I am a dancer when the tune
in my head makes me reach
and stretch and hop

or when notes from
nowhere shiver
through me and
shake me around.

I am a dancer when I bend like
grass in the wind
or lean against it, not giving in,
or when I flop down and turn
myself into a dash or a dot.

I am a dancer when I chase the tide

or let it run after me

or when I jump back from a wave
as it slaps the shore.

I am a dancer in my click-clacky shoes
or my slip-slappy ones

or in bare feet
that know how to
spring and twist

and twirl.

I am a dancer to the
steady drip-blip of rain,
the whisper of trees,
music carried on the air.

I am a dancer in the blowing leaves and autumn breezes,

and when I throw
a pitch or reach
for a catch.

Or quick-step to dribble a ball.

I am a dancer

with the leaping deer,
the wheeling hawk,
the soaring eagle,

the
darting
hummingbird,

the
jumping
frog.

Sometimes I am a dancer
to a silent throb
that makes me
spin and sway

and try to fly.

And whenever the beat
of the world's heart moves
into your fingers and toes
until you leap
and turn and take off,

you are a dancer too.